My Smart Puppy Guide:
How to Train Your Dog to Come

Sarah Wilson, M.A.

Cover design by goodlifeguide.com

Contents

Special thanks to my dear friends (some of whom are family, too) for your encouragement, questions, feedback, edits, and all-around support. Without you this book (and my life) would be so much less.

PREFACE

My friend Melissa and I walk together, chatting. The fall colors surround us and the grassy field spreads ahead, bending to the right. Pip, my beloved dog, is a speck in the distance as she follows the field out of sight. Since I have no idea what is around that curve, I call her. Instantly, a black blur streaks into view. Ears back, head extended— she floors it getting back to me.

I squat down. This sort of obedience, even after seven years together, deserves a major praise party. I clap my hands, cheering her on. Melissa shoots this picture over my shoulder.

Such moments embody why I teach my dogs to love coming when called. A great response like this one allows me to give Pip freedom while also helping me to keep her safe.

Also, training is fun for both of us. Too often, dog training is more like a military exercise or a science experiment than a play date between two friends. If we all have fun teaching our dogs, I believe more dogs will be trained—and trained well. So, go for it! Have fun!

Using the games in this book, Pip and I had a blast learning this together. Coming when called is an opportunity for us to enjoy each other. "Pip, Come!" are two of her favorite words. In fact, she loved them so much as a puppy that she took to pausing on our walks while I went ahead just so I would call her to me. "Pip, Come!" is a gift I have learned to give her, and her response is a gift she has learned to give to me.

I wrote this book to pass these gifts on—from Pip and me to your dog and you. I hope you have great fun learning together.

1

START HERE:
THE THREE PARTS
OF "COME!"

P eople say to me, "All I want is for my dog to come to me off leash," to which I respond, "That is like saying, 'All I want is for my child to play at Carnegie Hall.'" And how do you get to Carnegie Hall? As the old joke says, "*Practice, practice, practice!*"

In order to practice effectively, we have to know *what* to practice. Going out in the backyard, letting your dog loose, then calling him before either of you knows exactly what to do is, more often than not, practicing failure. It's like your child banging on the piano keys; he can do that forever but he'll never get any better, will he?

And his failure to improve isn't proof that he's difficult or stupid or even bad at piano. It's only proof that he hasn't gotten the coaching he needs to practice productively—and only productive practice produces progress.

Your dog learns what you mean by "Come" when he links those words with the action of coming to you. It doesn't matter how many dozens or even hundreds of times you've called him before. If you haven't known what to do and he hasn't actually done it, then it was just banging on the proverbial keys.

In order to teach "Come" so your dog understands, you need to see it as a three-step process in which your dog:

🐾 Turns away from whatever he is doing.

🐾 Runs back to you.

🐾 Stops within reach.

When your dog does each of these parts well, he will come when you call him. To create that result, we need to teach each piece separately. Here's a quick overview.

STEP 1 - TURNS AWAY

To come when called your dog must turn away from whatever he is doing and look back at you. And here's the rub: dogs do not know *how* to turn away from distractions. Really and truly—They. Do. Not. Know. How. Understanding this changed everything I did as a trainer.

Not only do dogs have no clue *how* to turn away from temptation, many dog breeds are bred not to. They were designed to stay relentlessly focused despite all distractions. You can, as you probably already know, yell "Come!" repeatedly without your dog even glancing in your direction. The good news? Dogs can—surprisingly quickly—learn how to turn away. Using the games here, they can even learn to see the distractions themselves as the *command* to look at you. For example, your dog sees a squirrel and looks up at you instead of lunging forward.

Stop laughing. It can happen.

In fact, that is a normal result of the games taught in Chapter 2. And once your dog sees something and starts to turn away on his own, your life (and his) just got better.

STEP 2 - RUNS BACK

In a perfect world, after your dog turns away from whatever he was doing, he races back to you like Pip did, at top speed without stopping along the way to sniff or wander. That is our goal, and that is exactly what the Chapter 3 games teach. They create desire in your dog to race all the way back to you. These games are fun for both ends of the leash and critical when it comes to "Come."

I use a dog's name when I call them. My logic is that dogs spend a lot of their life ignoring our general conversation. It seems fair to me that I alert them that I am talking to them directly by using their name at such moments. When talking about them to other people, I use nicknames. This effectively saves their name for when I really want their attention.

Throughout the book, I've used "Name, Come!" because that's the best way I can think of to remind you to use your dog's name in this way.

STEP 3 - STOPS WITHIN REACH

It is disappointing (and really annoying) when your dog races back to you, then continues right on past or dances playfully just out of reach. Some dogs seem to know—to the centimeter—just how long your arms are. Teaching a dog to stop close to you can easily be taught once you know how, and Chapter 4 gives you that know-how.

Let's get started!

2 TURNS AWAY

2

Pip spots the off-leash dog ahead and, without a word from me, turns her head to glance up at my face. I respond with a smile while praising her warmly as we turn in another direction. With Pip, as with hundreds of other dogs I have trained, that head turn away from the distraction and up at me has become nearly automatic. Seeing anything she finds interesting is the *command* for her to look up.

One of my favorite examples of this was the first time she saw a rabbit. When I moved to St. Louis, I had rabbits around my yard like most cities have pigeons in the parks. Pip had never seen a rabbit. When she did, she froze and then...looked at me. Even when I was in the house, I'd glance out the window and see her motionless in the backyard, glancing over her shoulder toward the door. Pip's a true believer (and a very funny dog). Now, I am not saying most dogs would take it to her level, but most will learn to check back with you before they lunge forward as a result of the two games you are about to learn.

This chapter is for you if your dog:

🐾 Gets focused on things and cannot stop.

🐾 Resists as you drag him away from things.

🐾 Is predatory.

🐾 Lies down when you try to get him away from something.

🐾 Drags you toward things.

🐾 Does not so much as flick an ear when you call him.

GAME:

HEAD TURNS

This game teaches your dog to turn his head away from distractions to look up at you. Once learned, this game provides the practice all dogs need to perfect this critical skill. As a professional dog trainer, I use it all the time. Not only does it help build an amazing response to "Come," but it also creates beautiful dog attention that can be useful in any situation where your dog is distracted.

What's the Point?

To come when called reliably, your dog **MUST** quickly and happily turn away from what he is doing and give his attention to you. This game builds that.

What Do You Need?

Your dog on a four-foot leash (yes it needs to be four feet) + a distraction like a non-rolling toy or large biscuit + small, really good treats in your hand or pocket + a quiet indoor place with plenty of room to back up.

How Do You Do It?

- ❧ Toss that distraction away from you a good distance—at least eight feet.

- ❧ The moment your dog shows interest in what you tossed (which might be right away), back away from the distraction.

- ❧ When the leash tightens, continue to back away while you squeeze/pulse the leash. (Squeeze/pulse is when you open and close your fingers, sort of like squeezing the water out of a sponge with one hand. There is no wrist, elbow or arm action—this is all finger flutters.)

- ❧ When he glances back at you, light up! Smile, praise, and encourage him to come to you.

- ❧ Feed him a couple of favorite small treats when he arrives then repeat.

- ❧ Once your dog gives you his attention quickly, then start adding in "Name, Come!" as you back up. Wait until you *know* your dog will turn away before you add the words.

Common Mistakes

- ❧ Standing still is the #1 mistake people make. Standing still keeps the dog within the zone of distraction, which means he'll probably just stand there focused on the item. You *must* back away. The more distance between that item and your dog, the more likely he is to tear himself away to reconnect with you.

- ❧ Turning away from the dog instead of backing away. Backing away means that you can see the moment your dog's head turns and mark it enthusiastically with praise. If you turn your back on your dog, you can't praise that critical moment.

- ❧ Not squeeze/pulsing the leash. Pulsing the leash prevents you from dragging your dog. Steady pulling on the leash will lead to dragging. Dragging means your dog's brain can still be 100 percent focused on the distraction. He can still be looking at it as you haul his body away, which defeats the whole purpose of this game. Don't drag your dog. Move backward and squeeze/pulse.

🐾 Getting too close to the distraction. Your goal is to react as soon as your dog's attention leaves you but before your dog does. Those ears go forward? You go backward!

It's Not Working!

🐾 Get farther away from the distraction.

🐾 Use a more boring distraction or better treats to reward your dog or both.

🐾 Pile on the praise.

🐾 As you back away, make a noise to try to get him to turn back to you.

It's Too Easy?

Excellent! Good job! To make things more challenging, you can move closer to the distraction, use a more tempting distraction or work outside (on leash). Or you can "raise the bar" by only giving food treats for his best response. Praise all efforts but only treat the best ones. Doing these things continually improves your dog's response by keeping him striving and engaged.

GAME: MOTHER MAY I?

With this game, you and your dog walk toward a distraction one step at a time. With each step, your dog stops when you stop and looks up at you. I love "Mother May I" because one round gives your dog many chances to practice looking away from the distraction and back up at you. As with any skill, the more successful repetition you do, the better you get. Same with your dog. This is a fantastic team-building exercise!

What's the Point?

We want the "Head Turn" to become automatic, right? This game strengthens that key part of "Come." It can be played indoors using any sort of distraction. Be creative; once you both know the ropes, use whatever distraction tempts your dog.

What Do You Need?

One hungry dog on leash + a quiet indoor area (halls can be great) + small treats your dog loves + a distraction your dog is interested in but not wild about.

How Do You Do It?

🐾 Toss that larger, somewhat boring treat/toy distraction away from you (the farther you toss it, the easier the game).

🐾 Have your dog sit. Stay still. Wait.

🐾 When he glances up at you, smile, praise, treat, and then take *one* step toward the temptation.

🐾 Stop. Have your dog sit. Stay still. Wait.

🐾 When he glances up at you, smile, praise, treat, and then take *one* step toward the temptation. Repeat this slow march toward the temptation.

🐾 When you get so close that you're worried about your dog lunging toward it, then back up and do a Head Turn; say "Name, Come!" as you squeeze/pulse the leash.

🐾 Get away from the item again, line back up, and play it again!

Common Mistakes

🐾 Walking toward the item without stopping. That's "Head Turns". "Mother May I" is one step at a time.

🐾 Getting so close the dog lunges at the item. Just back up sooner.

🐾 You let the dog grab the item off the floor. Nope. Allowing that keeps a part of your dog focused on the toy/treat at all times instead of 100 percent on you. If you want your dog to have the item at the end, pick it up and give it to him. The lesson to the dog? All good things come from looking at you!

It's Not Working!

🐾 Dog doesn't glance up at you. Either the temptation is too great or too close. Move farther away. Use something less enticing. Practice the "Head Turns" game some more.

🐾 Dog still doesn't glance up at you. Encourage him to look up by saying his name or making some noise. Stop the sound as soon as you can, but use it at first if you need it.

🐾 Dog STILL doesn't glance up. Are you giving him a treat when he is still looking at the distraction? Feed him only when he is looking back at you. *Always deliver the treat for the behavior you want.* You may need to put the treat to his nose and lure his head back to you the first couple of times, rewarding him when he is looking at you. But stop luring as soon as you can.

☙ Dog lunges toward the item. Get more distance. Use better treats to reward his attention. Don't get too close. Back away sooner. There's no rush; take your time.

It's Too Easy?

Fantastic! If you want to "raise the bar" then try more tempting items or practice outside. Or you can just pat yourself on the back. Good job!

3 RUNS BACK

3

The man issues a clear, confident "Come" to his dog, who responds instantly by pivoting, then running...in the *opposite direction*. Another friend's dog starts to sniff vigorously whenever "Come" is uttered.

What everyone wants to see when they call their dog is instant recognition then immediate energetic response. We want to see them racing back to us joyfully. Not only is this key to being able to keep your dog safe but that proof of connection, especially at a distance, feels deeply good. Seeing your dog coming when called—legs churning, ears flapping, running as fast as they can—is just one of the great moments. The games below help you create that.

This chapter is for you if your dog:

🐾 Looks at you when you call then goes back to what he was doing.

🐾 Starts heading your way when you call then gets distracted.

☙ Runs away from you when you call him.

☙ Meanders slowly in your general direction when you call.

GAME:

COME/SQUEAK!

Say "Name, Come!" then squeak a toy. Simple right? Actually, it is. Pip adores any toy that makes a noise so she loves playing this game. We play it still because it is fun. If your dog is as squeaker-happy as Pip, this game should work well for you.

What's the Point?

Playing this game correctly will earn you a dog racing back to you as fast as his legs can carry him when he hears "Name, Come!"

What Do You Need?

One toy-happy dog + one squeaky toy + a quiet indoor area + all other squeaky toys put away for the moment.

How Do You Do It?

☙ Hide the squeaker behind your back.

☙ Facing your dog say, "Name, Come!"

☙ *Then* smile/praise while you squeak that toy for all that you're worth!

🐾 When your dog arrives, continue to praise him as you toss the toy.

🐾 Allow him to play for a few seconds before you take away the toy.

🐾 Repeat.

Common Mistakes

🐾 Squeaking the toy *before* the command. This is tempting, but don't do it. That will only teach your dog to come to a squeaky sound—not a terrible thing, but not what we're aiming for. We want him to come when you call.

🐾 Working outside before the dog understands the game.

🐾 Trying to train this in a highly distracting situation like a dog park. In fact, you should <u>never </u>bring a squeaky toy to a dog park. It invites a fight.

🐾 Not playing with him for a minute or two after each response. This is his big reward, so let him enjoy it!

It's Not Working!

🐾 Your dog doesn't care about toys. Then how about treats? You can do the same routine with a bag or box of treats. Command, then shake box/bag! When the dog comes running, deliver a treat while you praise with delight.

🐾 Ignore your dog most of the time except when he comes to you (Free 'N Easy).

🐾 Keep your praise sincere but brief—a few seconds maximum.

🐾 Have a helper? Have them restrain your dog calmly as you move away. When he is intent on you, then have your helper release him.

🐾 Move away from him after you start to squeak so he'll follow you. Since dogs love to chase things that move, moving can focus them.

It's Too Easy?

FANTASTIC! Then play it from time to time for the fun of it. Oh, and if it works "too well" and your dog stays glued to you? That's okay. Every time you associate those words with that squeak, at any distance, even right next to you, you're doing a good thing.

GAME:

THROW-AWAY RECALLS

This is a fun activity where you throw a treat away from you, let the dog go get it, and then call your dog back for praise and better treats.

What's the Point?

This game practices all three of the behaviors that make up a solid "come when called" —head turns, running back and stopping within reach—quickly and conveniently.

What Do You Need?

One dog on leash + small, quickly-eaten treats + small, even better treats + a quiet spot.

How Do You Do It?

- 🐾 Toss one of those small, easily-eaten treats a few feet away. (A treat that contrasts with the floor helps your dog find it quickly.)

- 🐾 Let him go. The moment he eats it, call him back: "Name, Come!" and smile/praise.

- 🐾 When he arrives, smile, praise him, and give him an even better treat.

- 🐾 Repeat.

Common Mistakes

- 🐾 Tossing big treats that take time to chew.

- 🐾 Calling him *before* he gets to the thrown treat.

- 🐾 Calling him after he has finished and gotten distracted elsewhere.

- 🐾 Using the same treats as the one you threw.

- 🐾 Not praising warmly. If you let the treats do the rewarding then you are teaching your dog that treats are the most important thing. Bring yourself to your training! Smile! Praise!

It's Not Working!

- 🐾 Work in a more boring area like a hallway.

- 🐾 Reward him with treats he likes better than the one you tossed.

- 🐾 Train before his meals.

- 🐾 Is he on leash?

- 🐾 Practice a few more "Head Turns" then try again.

It's Too Easy?

You're on your way to a fantastic come when called! If you want to "raise the bar," you can toss a treat farther away, play this game outside (on leash), play inside off leash, have him sit when he comes back to you, or have him sit and look up at you ("Mother May I?") before you let him go get the tossed treat.

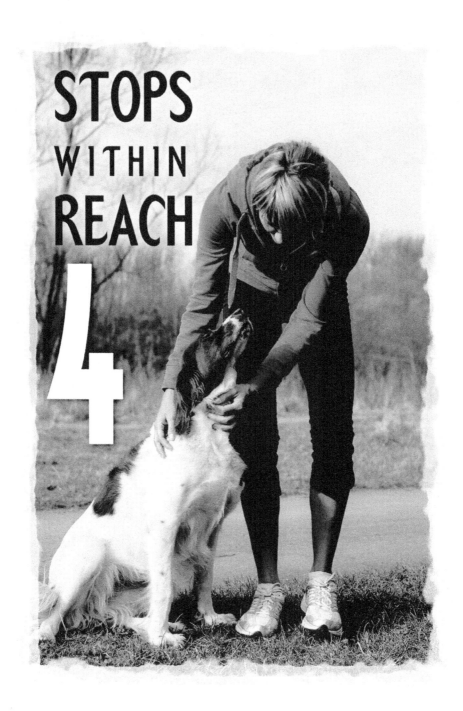

STOPS
WITHIN
REACH

4

4

Oh, that moment of disappointment. Your dog is racing back to you full tilt only to shoot right past you. Or, after trotting your way, he stops just out of reach. So frustrating!

The nice thing about this is that it is usually pretty easy to fix. Some daily practice before meals generally does the trick fairly quickly.

This chapter is for you if your dog:

🐾 Comes toward you then runs past.

🐾 Comes but stops out of reach.

🐾 Plays "keep away" when you try to catch him.

GAME:

CLOSE CALL

This will, as the name suggests, teach your dog to come close to you when you call him. It's a simple game with big results. If your dog enjoys treats, this game will work for you!

What's the Point?

To build a strong association between the words "Name, Come!" and treats.

What Do You Need?

One hungry dog + treats he likes.

How Do You Do It?

🐾 Have a few yummy treats in one hand.

🐾 With your dog near you, say, "Name, Come!" happily.

🐾 Immediately SMILE/PRAISE *before* giving a treat or two.

🐾 After a second or two, back up a step and repeat.

Common Mistakes

🐾 Treating before the words. Words come first!

🐾 Words/treats at the same moment. Words before treat!

🐾 Bending over as the dog approaches. Stand up straight, then feed with your hand held close to your body. Not only will this bring your dog in closer, but it protects your face from being smacked by an eager dog.

🐾 Dog jumping up on you to get the treats? Use less exciting treats. Tether your dog to a sturdy item so you can step back and away if he leaps at you. Work on your basic obedience—especially sitting—until this is resolved.

It's Not Working!

🐾 Use treats your dog likes better.

🐾 Play this game before his meals.

🐾 Move away from him before you call him, as dogs tend to follow things that move.

🐾 Move your hand as you offer the treat; let him chase it a bit. This can create a lot more interest in chase-loving dogs.

It's Too Easy?

You two are on a roll! Want to make it even more challenging? Store treats out of canine reach rather than holding them in your hand; put your treat hand behind your back or keep treats in your back pocket out of sight.

GAME: GOTCHA!

This game teaches your dog to allow you to put your hand on his collar.

What's the Point?

Being able to catch your dog, which is the entire point of "Come."

What Do You Need

One dog with a non-tightening, regular flat buckle or clip collar on + treats he likes.

How Do You Do It?

- 🐾 Start with your dog near you, on leash if necessary.

- 🐾 Have a treat in one hand.

- 🐾 Say, "Name, Come!" and reach toward his collar with your treat-free hand.

- 🐾 As that hand touches the collar, give him the treat with the other.

- 🐾 Now stand up and ignore him for a few seconds, then repeat.

- 🐾 Reach/treat; reach/treat. Keep it up until your dog is *hoping* you'll reach for his collar.

    CAVEAT: *If your dog growls at any time for any reason during any training, please seek qualified professional assistance ASAP. Talk to his veterinarian, too, as sometimes dogs get growly because they are uncomfortable or sick.*

Common Mistakes

- 🐾 Moving too fast or suddenly and spooking the dog.

- 🐾 Dragging him by the collar. Doing that, especially when you are upset, can make him leery of anyone taking hold of it.

- 🐾 You give the treat before you reach for the collar.

It's Not Working!

🐾 Hold a delicious treat with back of your hand resting on your leg so your dog must come close to get it.

🐾 Reach more slowly.

🐾 Back away as your dog approaches. If you want him to follow you, move!

🐾 Reward him as you start to reach; slowly build up to touching his collar.

🐾 For a few days, feed him all his food as rewards for this game.

It's Too Easy?

Nicely done! Reaching for his collar faster, from different angles or fussing with the collar a bit *before* you deliver the treat takes this game to the next level.

5

THREE COMMON MISTAKES TO STOP MAKING

5

We all make mistakes training dogs. I've made plenty myself. Mistakes are a part of learning a new skill. Each error you recognize and change is a badge of your growth.

Here are three common things people do, why each action creates problems, and what to do instead.

1. Producing treats *after* your dog ignores you.

2. Scolding your dog when he finally comes to you.

3. Doing something he finds unpleasant when you've called him to you.

Any of those sound familiar? If yes, you're not alone. I've helped thousands of people make better choices. Let me explain why these things do more harm than good:

1) Producing treats after your dog ignores you.

Your dog doesn't budge when you call him, so you hustle off, get a treat and hold it out. You call him again. He sees the treat. He comes. Success? Noooo...that's a problem in the making.

From your dog's perspective, this is what happened: NOT responding caused you to go get a cookie. In human terms, it's as if you ask your child to take out the trash, he ignores you so you offer him a $10 bill. He then takes out the trash. What will happen the next time you ask him to do this chore?

I'll promise you that he'll wait for the $10—*at least* the $10. It's the same with your dog. I've worked with dozens of dogs who learned that if they stood at a distance and did not move, their people did move—right to the cookie jar!

If your dog doesn't respond, either he wasn't ready for this level of distraction or he didn't understand what you wanted, so go get him—calmly, neutrally, but with no cookie in sight. Time to sharpen your skills by playing more of the games you've learned in this book.

> INSTEAD: If you call him and he does not respond, go get him! If you cannot get him, try running away from him clapping and sounding VERY happy. That sort of movement + enthusiasm often does the trick. Once you have him, commit to practicing on a leash until this problem is a thing of the past.

2) Scolding your dog when he finally comes to you.

You've been calling and calling your dog with no success. You're so frustrated when he finally arrives (or you finally catch him), that you scold him. The problem is—he's a dog. What he learns is that coming to you/being caught causes bad things to happen.

> INSTEAD: No matter what—and I mean no matter what—if your dog comes to you (or allows you to catch him), you praise him. Or if you can't pull that off, then at least be silent. Don't punish him for letting you near him.

3) Doing something he finds unpleasant when you've called him to you.

Your dog needs a bath or you need to clip on his leash to leave the park. You call him; you get right down to business when he arrives. Next time you call your dog, he's a bit slower to come to you because he really doesn't know if this is going to be a happy time or not.

> INSTEAD: Always praise your dog, and make it a happy occasion when he comes to you. If you need to do something he won't like, go to him calmly and cheerfully, get him, and then do what needs to be done. If you must do something negative after he comes to you (such as leashing him up to exit the dog park), take a few seconds to praise him warmly before you do the unpleasant thing. Those are seconds very well spent.

6 ON-LEASH PRACTICE

6

As every dog lover knows, getting response outside is harder, at first, than getting it inside. My rule: You'll lose 50 percent of your inside response when you move your training outside. So, if you're running at about 60 percent inside, you'll be at 30 percent outside initially.

Things can improve quickly with a bit of on-leash practice. Play the same games. Start in a calm area, then progress to busier or new places. Beginning work on a paved surface can make things easier, too. Be extra generous with your praise and use especially good treats that your dog only gets for listening outside.

Be sure to practice *on* leash anywhere you want your dog to respond *off* leash, including the backyard or the park. (Don't use dog treats in the dog park—that's asking for trouble.)

> <u>Hint:</u> *Notice when the leash tightens during training; that signals something you need to practice more. Only when the leash is loose throughout these games are you ready to consider going off leash.*

FREE 'N EASY

Reward your dog whenever he comes to you. Two minutes ago, Pip smiled at me as she approached. I smiled back, and we shared a few moments of happy connection as she wagged and I stroked. Just because something is easy doesn't mean it doesn't work. Use these life moments to build your dog's simple enjoyment of coming to you.

What is It?

When your dog comes to you on his own, you make the most of it.

What's the Point?

To build your dog's positive feeling about coming to you, while teaching you how to heap on praise in a brief but effective way.

What Do You Need?

To notice your dog + a few seconds to really enjoy the moment.

How Do You Do It?

- 🐾 Is your dog coming to you? Smile, praise, celebrate for about 5 seconds, and then...ignore him.

- 🐾 Try to end an interaction before your dog does. Leave him wanting more!

Common Mistakes

- 🐾 Missing the opportunities or thinking it is too easy to be "real training." Missing these moments isn't a crisis; it's just a wasted chance to teach your pup. Why waste a chance?

❧ You overwhelm or annoy your dog. Watch your dog. Does he look away, lean away or walk away when you praise him? If yes, time to change some things. Read on.

It's Not Working!

❧ Your dog never comes to you? Hmmm....try ignoring him completely unless he heads your way.

❧ Watch how he reacts to your touch. If he turns away or moves away, try being gentler, quitting sooner, or stroking the way his fur grows. Some dogs like to be touched in ways we are not used to touching. Once you touch him in ways he enjoys, things should improve.

❧ After brief praise, move away from sensitive/shy dogs. Such dogs can become tense when they come close and stay close. You moving away before they do is a good reward for their effort making them more confident about approaching you next time. This is a great tip for rescue/abused dogs.

It's Too Easy?

Good. Enjoy the happy connection you have with your dog.

GAME:

EAST/WEST

In this game, you change direction when your dog gets distracted. Here's one of my general rules: I do not follow a dog who is dragging me. Why? Because by following I am *training* him to drag me, telling him by following him that when he is distracted enough he can just forget about me! Ummmm...no. Instead (and as always), I reward turning away from distractions back to me.

What is It?

This is an outdoor, on-a-walk, advanced level of the indoor "Head Turns" game. Play it outside only when you are both excellent at head turns inside.

What's the Point?

To teach your dog to pay attention to you. To turn and follow you quickly with no resistance. If your dog won't come away from distractions quickly on leash, what hope is there off?

What Do You Need?

One dog on a four-foot leash + time in your day to play + some treats + faith enough to try.

How Do You Do It?

- ❧ As you're walking along, as soon as you see those ears focus forward, you turn and walk the other way.

- ❧ If you feel any tension on the leash, you squeeze/pulse as you keep moving.

- ❧ When your dog catches up, praise! Treat! Stop and celebrate for about 5 seconds then proceed with your walk.

- ❧ Dog getting good at that? Excellent! Now add the word. When you go the other way, say, "Name, Come!" and proceed as usual. When your dog catches up—pause. Smile/praise, stroke, treat, and then continue on.

Common Mistakes

🐾 Waiting for your dog instead of moving while squeeze/pulsing.

🐾 Following your dog instead of turning away.

🐾 Dragging your dog instead of squeeze/pulsing.

🐾 Not celebrating your dog's success.

It's Not Working!

Some dogs have a hard time coming away from distraction, but if they cannot come away from it on leash you cannot expect it off leash—so go back to "Head Turns" and turn, turn, turn, turn!

It's Too Easy?

Terrific! Keep practicing. Work hard not to follow your dog when he drags you. Changing such moments into coming-when-called practice has many benefits, including saving your shoulders a lot of wear and tear.

7

GAMES
FOR TWO
PEOPLE

7

There are many games two (or more) people can play with dogs that strengthen the dogs' desire to come when called. Here are two of those games. Having another person to help is not a requirement of any kind, but if you happen to have a helper, why not make the most of it and have some fun at the same time?

GAME:

PUPPY PING-PONG

Your dog or puppy racing between you and a friend? Okay, that's both great training and darn fine entertainment.

What is It?

Your dog runs back and forth as you and your helper(s) call.

What's the Point?

Gives much needed practice for reliably coming when called with enthusiasm.

What Do You Need?

One hungry dog + a willing friend + treats in hand + inside location + not-too-slippery flooring.

How to Play:

🐾 In a quiet area (a hallway is a perfect place to start), sit (for small or young dogs) or stand a few feet away from each other.

🐾 Person #1 calls the pup, then enthusiastically praises and claps her hands whether or not the dog is moving yet. This is to encourage the dog, just as cheering encourages a runner to the finish line. When the dog gets to her, she'll heap on a few seconds of praise and give a couple of tiny, yummy treats.

🐾 Then she takes hands off the dog and ignores him. At that moment, person #2 calls the dog enthusiastically. If the dog doesn't come, that person goes to him, shows him the treat, and backs away with the pup following. Praise and treat. Then ignore.

🐾 Person #1 calls again.

🐾 Your pup will quickly catch on to this game, racing back and forth happily. If he gets *too* good at it and starts racing back and forth before anyone calls, just wait him out. When he pauses, the person farthest away calls him.

Common Mistakes

🐾 The person who just treated the puppy/dog does not ignore him when the other person calls.

🐾 The person who just treated the dog tries to help the dog by talking to him and pointing to the other person, which simply engages the dog further. Once you reward, stand up and look away. Put your hands behind your back. Message to the dog: Nothing more from me. Go to the person calling you.

🐾 Person calling waits for the dog to respond *before* praising. In this game, use the praise to help create the response.

It's Not Working!

🐾 Start closer together.

🐾 Start with a hungrier pup.

🐾 Start in a more boring area.

🐾 Put the treat to your dog's nose, then praise as you back up to your start spot. Treat there.

🐾 Praise more enthusiastically.

It's Too Easy?

Your dog runs to whomever calls quickly and happily? Excellent! You can make it more of a challenge by walking to a new location when the pup is racing toward the other person. This requires the pup to listen and think.

GAME:

HIDE-AND-SEEK

I love Hide-and-Seek with dogs; it brings out the kid in me. It's fun to hide and even more fun to have my dog excitedly find me.

What is it?

Your helper restrains your dog as you go hide, then you call him. You can play this solo by simply ducking out of sight when your dog is otherwise occupied.

What's the Point?

This creates an exciting search situation for your dog. Also, your praise is likely to be sincere and delighted when he finds you. Dogs respond well to that sort of praise (don't we all?).

How to Play:

- ❧ Have your helper restrain your dog on leash or by the collar. (As always, this assumes that your dog accepts this easily. If he does not, do other games and find good local hands-on training help.)

- ❧ Staying inside the house, you go out of the room and "hide" in plain view.

- ❧ Call your dog; your helper releases at that moment.

- ❧ You continue to praise happily, encouraging your dog to find you.

❀ When he does, celebrate! Praise! Use treats or toys if you need them but many dogs are plenty inspired just by the fun of it all. Repeat.

Common Mistakes

❀ Falling silent after you call the dog.

❀ Hiding in too hard a place too soon.

❀ Your assistant talks to the dog, keeping your dog focused on her.

❀ You don't really celebrate when your dog finds you.

It's Not Working!

❀ If your dog isn't looking for you, take better treats or toys with you. Show your dog you have them, then move away.

❀ Praise and keep praising as your dog looks for you. If you're quiet, he can lose focus.

❀ Play in a boring area where nothing else is happening.

❀ Ask others in your home to ignore the dog when you're playing this.

❀ Have him on leash and have your assistant help him get to you. Be sure your assistant ignores him when you're praising.

It's Too Easy?

There are many ways to make this fun game a bit harder for your dog: make less noise when he is searching for you or hide in harder spots. Always keep in mind not to teach him something in play that you don't want him doing any other time, so no hiding spots that encourage digging, scratching, or climbing on things that shouldn't be climbed on.

8 SIMPLE SOLUTIONS TO THREE COMMON PROBLEMS

8

P uppies are not born understanding our language—we teach them. So, everything your dog knows about "Come" he learned from one of us. Everything. If we don't like what they know, that's our doing.

No matter. We begin again today. The good news? Everything he needs to know to get better also comes from us. And only us. He can't learn good habits from TV or reading this book or talking on the playground with other dogs. All improvement comes from direct practice with us. So, it's time for on-leash, make-it-happen, "Good-Dog!" practice.

> *How much he improves depends on us. How much effort are you willing to put in?*
>
> *How about five minutes a day?*

Put in five minutes a day. You'll be surprised at what you can accomplish in that focused five minutes! I bet you'll be proud, too. And you should be. When you invest those five minutes, you are investing in your dog's safety and freedom.

Dog training done this way, using the games and techniques you learn here, is one of the most rewarding activities *for humans* I have found. Doing it is fun. Seeing the results even more fun.

Everyone has problems with the "Come" command from time to time. Here are three common issues and how to solve them using the knowledge you now have.

WON'T LET YOU CATCH HIM

Oh, this frustrating problem inevitably seems to crop up when you have the least amount of time to deal with it. Some dogs are real pros, slipping out of reach expertly and, I swear, laughing as they do it.

What sort of problem is this? Well, the dog isn't stopping within reach so you know what to do!

CLOSE CALL

Play this all over the place until you have your dog's focus when he hears the magic words: "Name, Come!" and he comes right over to you when he hears them.

GOTCHA!

Exactly as above, play this everywhere you can—inside and out, distracted and calm—until your dog not only *allows* you to reach for his collar, but *wants* you to. When that happens, you will have created true success.

FREE 'N EASY

We need to change your dog's mind about coming to you—all the way to you—so using moments when he is coming to you on his own is a powerful tool. Really give of yourself when you notice this happening. Smile and praise warmly, but then quit while you're ahead. When you see him speeding up a bit when he's headed your way, add in "Name, Come!"

> **Emergency!** *Your dog has run off; he's in danger and is not letting you near him. This is no time to*

attempt training; this is the time to get your dog! Each of these acts of pure desperation has worked for me at one time or another; I hope they work for you!

TRY:

🐾 Running away from the dog clapping and laughing.

🐾 Running parallel, laughing and clapping.

🐾 Starting the car.

🐾 Shaking a box of dog treats.

🐾 Start feeding and loudly praising another dog.

🐾 Start tossing a favorite toy around by yourself or with a friend.

🐾 Firmly ask for a "sit" or "down" (sometimes that works, don't know why).

🐾 Focus on something on the ground very, very intently. Poke at it; stare at it. (I caught a loose Rottweiler in Prospect Park, NY, that way; he just got curious about what I was doing and walked over.)

PS: Running after the dog usually just makes him run away *faster*.

WON'T COME INSIDE

Your dog will not come back inside. The more of a rush you're in, the more of a catch-me-if-you-can bozo he is. This upsets you. Your stress is completely obvious to your dog, making it even *less* likely he'll come through the door.

Why does this happen? There are many reasons; the most common two are the result of cause and effect. The dog comes back inside in the morning and that causes you to crate him and leave. At least, that's the math he does in his canine mind. Simple dog solution: Don't come back inside. The other cause is you going to get a great treat when he refuses to come in. Message to dog: Staying outside = great treats. Okay!

No matter the exact cause, let's just fix it. Here are the three games I'd use to get your dog thinking differently.

HEAD TURNS

For this issue, play this in the open doorway. Put him on leash then let him out (hold on to the leash). Now close the door and count to ten. Open the door, say: "Name, Come!" then back up. Squeeze/pulse if you need, too. The moment his front feet cross the threshold burst into praise. Let him come to you; don't go to him. Now, celebrate. Let him know exactly how pleased you are. Praise for a few seconds then repeat.

COME/SQUEAK!

This is my favorite game for resolving this issue. Play it on leash as above but, instead of backing up when you open the door, you call him and then squeak a toy excitedly. When he comes in, close the door as you toss the toy into the house. Let him play with it for a minute or so excitedly, then take the toy, let him outside, and repeat.

GOTCHA!

Also at the threshold, play "Gotcha!" so that, even if he has a hard time coming all the way in, he won't have a hard time allowing himself to be caught.

SNIFFS ON HIS WAY BACK TO YOU, OR APPEARS NOT TO HEAR YOU

While this may seem to be pure distraction (and sometimes it is), it can be a sign of stress. If he has any history of anyone getting angry with him when he gets to them or if he's a rescue dog, then getting frustrated with him will only make sniffing around worse. This can lead to a horrendous cycle where he dawdles, you get frustrated, he becomes more concerned, he dawdles more, and you are sure he knows better and is just doing this to upset you, so you become more frustrated...

Here's a very useful dog training rule: *If the behavior you are working on is getting worse: STOP! Whatever you're trying isn't working. Review the exact issues you're having, then play the dog games that address them.*

Here are three games I suggest focusing on:

FREE 'N EASY

Time to regroup. We need to reprogram his response to "Come" from *uh-oh* to *I love it!* To do that, use every chance you get to reward him for coming to you. If he seems hesitant, try backing away as you praise him. That draws many dogs to you much more effectively than standing in one place.

THROW-AWAY RECALLS

This game allows you to repeatedly practice all three parts of coming when called—turning away from whatever he is doing, coming back to you and then stopping within reach—in your living room. It's a great game that gives your dog a lot of valuable behavioral mileage doing happy, speedy coming when called.

PUPPY PING-PONG

Requires a helper, but this is a great game to build enthusiasm and consistency in any dog and to rebuild trust in a dog who's had it shaken a bit.

9

PUTTING IT ALL TOGETHER

9

Ready for more advanced work? Excellent! Next steps forward are either more distraction around the dog or more distance from the dog. Try to work one new thing at a time until you are confident in your dog's understanding, then you can brave working distraction and distance together.

For more distraction, go to more exciting areas such a parking lot, outside a dog run, or a large pet supply store. Practice on your regular leash (I use a four-footer). Make sure you have room to play your games; bring extra delicious dog treats and play away.

Expect things to be messier than at home. That's normal. Treat problems as information. Note the areas of trouble so you can practice that piece back at home. Have faith. You'll progress quicker than you may fear.

As his experience builds, your dog will adjust more quickly to new places with less and less drop in responsiveness. In each new location/situation, create success by practicing what you both know; you'll soon have your dog working with you again.

If that does not happen then you've probably gone too far too fast. Go back to calmer ground. Practice with a range of stationary distractions to give your dog more successful practice. Do extra practice with the parts your dog is weak in. Then try again.

It's really like any other sport. You play the game a bit, find a spot you need to improve in, practice that separately, and then try again when you're better than you were. Dogs benefit from the same approach.

Always remember that, unlike us, dogs do not have any idea about the goal of the game. When you pick up a baseball bat and step to the plate, you know exactly what you're trying to accomplish. When you practice these games with your dog, your dog has no idea about your plan. They need extra repetitions before the light bulb goes on. The fact that it goes on so relatively quickly is a tribute to the brilliance of dogs.

Distance is the next challenge. When I start to work distance, I use a longer leash—first a six-foot and then a ten-foot long line. I like those because they are easier to handle and less prone to tangling than longer lines while still giving the dog more room to explore.

For long-line work I wear gloves and hold one hand out in front to control the leash and the other I use to manage the line as needed. Long lines are always clipped to a well-fitted flat collar—not a training collar of any kind, a head halter nor a harness. I work in safe, low-traffic areas, allowing the dogs to sniff and explore. I do exactly the same games on that as I did already on a short leash.

If you are lucky enough to have access to a safe and secure fenced area, you can play these games again but with your dog dragging the leash. The more places you play these games, the better your dog will understand what is expected and the better his response will become.

Lastly, the bedrock foundation of the sort of come when called that Pip has is my day-to-day relationship with her. Her habit of responding to me is built in every daily interaction. If she doesn't listen consistently in the kitchen, how can I expect her to listen reliably outside?

Dogs are our mirrors. If we are not consistent, they are not consistent. If we let things slide, they do the same. They are not "bad" for doing so; they just believe what we teach them and we teach them all the time.

Now you have the tools to build a wonderful response to the words, "Name, Come!" My hope is that you enjoy the journey together, learn more about your dog and yourself in the process and that your dog learns to come when called consistently and joyfully.

Happy training!

10 CONCLUSION AND LINKS

10

Thank you for reading this book. Thank you for learning and trying new things. Thank you for caring so much about your dog. I am a huge fan of people like you. I always have been, but my admiration grows as the years go on.

I hope you have found this approach and these games helpful. If you like my methods and my style, here is a link to my Amazon page. I'm writing more books all the time.

http://www.amazon.com/Sarah-Wilson/e/B000APGEVE/

WIKIPEDIA PAGE: Sarah Wilson (dog trainer)

http://en.wikipedia.org/wiki/Sarah_Wilson_28dog_trainer29

LIST OF BLOGS

http://sarahwilsondogexpert.com/
http://dogbeds-info.com/
http://doggifts-info.com/
http://dogcrates-info.com/
http://dogcarriers-info.com/
http://dogtoys-info.com/
http://dogtreats-info.com/
http://doghouses-info.com/
http://dogtreadmills-info.com/

JOIN ME ON SOCIAL MEDIA

Twitter https://twitter.com/MySmartPuppy
Facebook https://www.facebook.com/MySmartPuppyPage
G+ https://plus.google.com/+SarahWilsonMySmartPuppy
Pinterest http://www.pinterest.com/mysmartpuppy

Made in the USA
Coppell, TX
22 June 2020